Take Care of Yourself

Your Body Belongs to You

by Ashley Richardson

PEBBLE

a capstone imprint

Published by Pebble, an imprint of Capstone.
1710 Roe Crest Drive, North Mankato, Minnesota 56003
capstonepub.com

Library of Congress Cataloging-in-Publication Data
Names: Richardson, Ashley, author.
Title: Your body belongs to you / Ashley Richardson.
Description: North Mankato, Minnesota : Pebble, [2022]. | Series: Take care of yourself | Includes bibliographical references and index. | Audience: Ages 5–8 | Audience: Grades K–1 | Summary: "The important topic of personal boundaries and respect are introduced to young readers. Straightforward text and examples help readers learn how to advocate for themselves and who to ask when they need help"—Provided by publisher.
Identifiers: LCCN 2021029813 (print) | LCCN 2021029814 (ebook) | ISBN 9781663976772 (hardcover) | ISBN 9781666326918 (paperback) | ISBN 9781666326925 (pdf) | ISBN 9781666326949 (kindle edition)
Subjects: LCSH: Security (Psychology) in Children—Juvenile literature. | Personal space—Juvenile literature. | Interpersonal relations—Juvenile literature. | Respect for persons—Juvenile literature.
Classification: LCC BF723.S22 R53 2022 (print) | LCC BF723.S22 (ebook) | DDC 304.2/3—dc23
LC record available at https://lccn.loc.gov/2021029813
LC ebook record available at https://lccn.loc.gov/2021029814

Image Credits
Getty Images: MachineHeadz, 17, SDI Productions, 15, Terry Vine, 7; Shutterstock: Anna Golant (design element) throughout, Dmytro Zinkevych, 14, Kenishirotie, 20, LightField Studios, 13, Monkey Business Images, 6, pixelheadphoto digitalskillet, 18, Serhii Bobyk, 19, Tai Dundua, 21, wavebreakmedia, Cover, 5, 11, wee dezign, 9

Editorial Credits
Editor: Erika L. Shores; Designer: Heidi Thompson; Media Researcher: Jo Miller; Production Specialist: Tori Abraham

Printed in the United States   4863

Table of Contents

Words in **bold** are in the glossary.

You're in Charge

You make choices every day. You can choose to do a silly dance. You can decide to stand still. You can choose to run really fast. You can decide to run slow. You can choose to hug a friend. You can decide to high-five instead. You are the boss of your body.

Personal Space

You **interact** with people every day. You talk to teachers and classmates. You might play with friends. Interacting can involve sharing personal space. This is the area around you. Hugs share personal space. Sitting in a circle does too.

Sharing personal space can be a sign of friendship or **affection**. We often touch, hug, or stand close to people we care about.

Sometimes people don't want others in their personal space. Maybe a classmate is tired. Maybe a family member is not feeling well. There are many reasons to want extra space and **privacy**.

It is important to give people personal space when they want it. It shows we **respect** them and their needs.

Setting Boundaries

You are waiting in line for the bus. A friend stands too close and steps on your foot. You ask your friend not to stand so close. You just set a **boundary**.

Boundaries are rules that tell people what you do and don't like. It is important to talk about things that make you uncomfortable.

11

You can set all kinds of boundaries.
It is OK to tell someone not to touch your
hair. It is OK to tell someone you don't want
a hug. You can tell someone not to tickle
you. You have the right to say you don't
like to be touched a certain way.

Setting boundaries doesn't mean be
rude. You can be firm and **polite**. Say "No,
thank you" and "Please don't do that."

Respecting Boundaries

You took your friend's pencil without asking. You didn't think it was a big deal. But your friend is mad. Ask **permission** before taking something. It shows respect for someone else's personal space.

People should respect your personal space too. Did your friends do something you don't like? Stop and think. Did you tell them you don't like their behavior? If not, use your words to tell them.

Is someone doing something to you that is unsafe or harmful? Is hitting or pushing involved? Find a grown-up to help you.

There are parts of your body that are more private than others. These body parts are the ones covered by a swimsuit. These private parts belong to you. If anyone tries to look at or touch them, tell an adult you trust right away.

17

Boundaries can be different each day. You like lots of hugs some days. Other days you may not want any.

Boundaries can change from person to person. Maybe you like hugs from family members but not from teachers. You may like to hold hands with a friend but never with someone you just met. It is OK to feel different around different people. Your body belongs to you!

Your Personal Space

It is important to talk about what is and isn't
OK inside your personal space. So, let's practice!

What You Need:

- paper
- pencils, markers, or crayons
- a partner

What You Do:

1. On the paper, draw a big circle. The inside of the circle is your personal space.

2. Now make a "yes" list. Think of three things you don't mind in your personal space (hugs, high fives). Write or draw them in the circle.

3. Next make a "no" list. Pick three things you don't like in your personal space (tickling, holding hands). Write or draw them outside the circle.

4. With a partner, talk about your "yes" and "no" lists. Practice politely saying you don't like something.

Glossary

affection (uh-FEK-shuhn)—a great liking for someone or something

boundary (BOUN-dur-ee)—a rule you make about the kinds of behaviors that aren't OK in your personal space

interact (in-tur-AKT)—to have action between people, groups, or things

permission (pur-MISH-uhn)—the OK to do something

polite (puh-LITE)—having good manners

privacy (PRY-vuh-see)—the state of being alone or being away from other people

respect (ri-SPEKT)—to believe in the quality and worth of others and yourself

Read More

Brian, Rachel. *Consent (for Kids!): Boundaries, Respect, and Being in Charge of You.* New York: Little, Brown and Company, 2020.

Schuette, Sarah L. *Stranger Safety.* North Mankato, MN: Pebble, 2020.

Internet Sites

KidsHealth: How to Handle Abuse
kidshealth.org/en/kids/handle-abuse.html

KidSmartz: Tell a Trusted Adult
youtu.be/YSZ22sx--_4

KidSmartz: Tell People No
youtu.be/lT1COP9EMIo

Index

About the Author

Ashley Richardson writes fiction, poetry, and creative nonfiction. She enjoys reading all kinds of books and lives in the Midwest with a houseful of plants. For fun, Ashley loves to inline skate in the park.